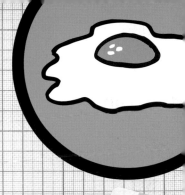

what is this?

Doubletakes

PICTURE PUZZLES WITH A TWIST !

By the lovely people @ The Backland Studio

CARLTON
BOOKS

Contents

Curious Characters

a rocket?

a plane?

Does it move quickly? Faster than a speeding bullet . . .

a shark with flippers?

9

It's a superhero
with a fence post!

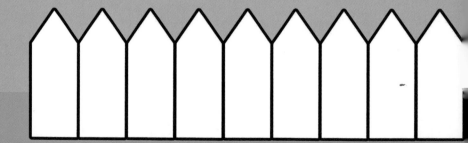

Ever heard the saying 'Never judge a book by its cover'? Well, it couldn't be truer of this lot!

Can you make out who's who . . . or what's who . . . or who's what?

Hot and buttered? More like hot and bothered . . .

It's a chef bending down to the oven!

A baby in facepaint? Don't be a dummy...

It's a cowboy in a bath!

What is this? Turn over to guess...

13

what is this?

A bashful worm in a bow tie? You must be joking . . .

It's a clown trapped in lift doors!

A woodlouse on the beach? Think inject, not insect . . .

It's a surgeon putting on his mask!

what is this?

A short nail? Or a short male?....

It's a small bald man hiding in a dustbin!

16

Does it need water? It's getting some . . . .

It's an elf diving down a well!

green worms?

a plant?

17

Is it the right address? More like in a dress . . . .

It's a woman carrying a tin bath on her head!

Time for an ice cream? He might prefer one . . .

It's a man sucking a lemon!

a ball ~~ball rolling into a~~ eating into a bowl of dessert?

19

Have you seen the light? Rubbish! . . .

It's a priest with a bin on his head!

20

Do these taste good? They're great with mushrooms ...

It's five elves in a boat!

21

Is it dangerous? Positively deadly . . .

It's a girl falling down a lift shaft!

Is it made of metal? You're on the right track . . .

It's a knight wearing a stripy jumper!

23

what is this?

A wall hiding a cat? Try a pair of hats! ...

It's two witches in a public lavatory!

24

Hitting the right notes? Or hitting their heads? . . .

It's stilt-walkers approaching a low bridge!

liquorice lollipops?

Is it a cosy? Yes, in a way . . . .

It's a bald man trying on his new Christmas jumper!

Christmas fare? More fairground mishap! …

It's a bowling ball hitting a man!

what is this?

Can't see for looking? Don't lose your head! . . .

It's an invisible priest!

Would a boy scout use it? It's more wobble than woggle . . .

It's a Canadian Mountie climbing a tree!

a stick with a watch on??

29

Animal Antics

30

a Kangaroo?

Is it a cute creature? Well, it's under acute stress...

a mouse?

It's a rabbit walking the plank!

Can you spot the crazy creatures in these images?

Whatever they are, they're not what they seem!

Turn over for more animal antics!

Does it go 'Quack'? More like 'Oof! Oof!'...

It's a rabbit doing sit-ups!

Would it give you a shock? Well, it would be a surprise . . .

It's an octopus throwing a bar stool!

35

what is this?

Can you hide in it? Sometimes too well ...

It's a sheep lost in an orchard!

Is it nice with ice? Well, it's wise to wear one in the cold ...

It's a bear in a balaclava!

36

A sparkling drink? Try love in pink! ...

It's two piglets kissing in the moonlight!

37

what is this?

Can you sleep in it? Well, he's dropped off . . .

It's a bird relaxing in the bath!

Shocked bunnies? No, but they're not chilled either . . .

It's two seagulls sunbathing!

Is it good with fries? Maybe, but this one prefers bread ...

It's a snake snuggling a baguette!

40

Is it smug? It's achieved quite a feat! . . .

It's a seal balancing on a tree stump!

what is this?

Would it scratch you? Only if you interrupt . . .

It's a beaver raiding a dustbin!

42

A bird's eye view of something? Too right . . .

It's a parrot looking through a telescope!

43

what is this?

Crowns and bushes? Or goes and flushes?......

It's a duck on the toilet!

It looks fishy . . . . It likes fishy . . .

It's a kitten holding a pool ball!

45

what is this?

Fancy putting this in your mouth? Jump right in . . .

It's a centipede on a diving board!

Will it keep its foot dry? It might if it had one . . .

It's a python sneaking under a grand piano!

Does it like to keep busy? Not if it can help it. . . .

It's a cat yawning!

Does it peep? More like 'Cheep! Cheep!' ...

It's a budgie in a canoe!

49

what is this?

Is it bushy? It could do with a trim . . .

It's a goose with an afro!

50

A wonderful gift? Well she's enjoying it . . .

It's a butterfly eating a slice of battenburg!

51

what is this?

Feeling down? Quite the opposite . . .

It's two jellyfish on a trampoline!

52

Would you eat it with a spoon? Not if you could help it . . . It's a duck falling into a blender.

Is it a board? It will be at lift-off . . .

It's a dog in an astronaut helmet!

Is it fun to play? This pair thinks so . . .

It's two dogs chasing a squash ball!

Is it watching something? Two things, actually . . .

It's a tadpole babysitting frogspawn!

55

what is this?

Does it go 'Chop! Chop!'? More like 'Splat!' ...

It's a bat flying into a pole!

Does it turn? No, it's wedged in . . . .

It's a spider in a barrel!

Does it make scores? Don't be daft, it can't write music!

It's a clam playing a harmonica!

58

Is it washing? You could call it that . . .

It's a penguin licking its plate clean!

what is this?

Do you find it in the kitchen? Looks like they did . . . .

It's ants carrying a loaf of bread!

60

A nice juicy fruit? It's not even a vegetable! . . .

It's a greenfly on a bean bag!

what is this?

What goes up must come down . . . .

It's a bird falling off its perch!

they pop? They might if they don't stop . . .

It's maggots eating spaghetti!

Is it a hill? More like a bump . . .

It's a giraffe walking under a low bridge!

63

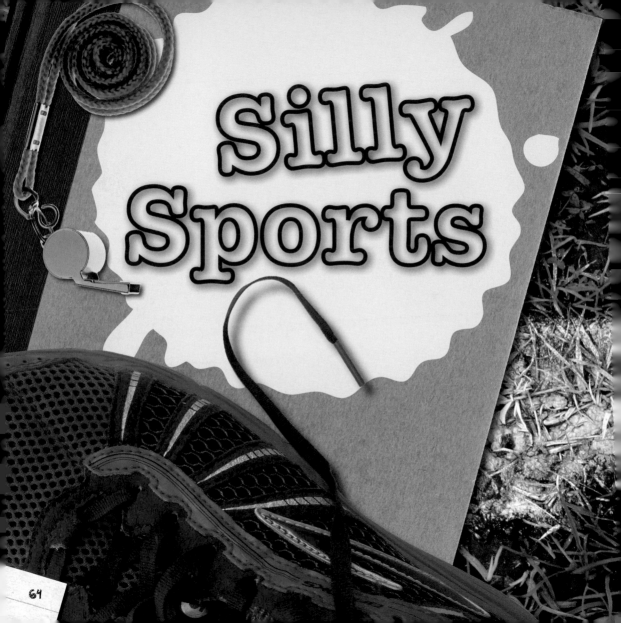

Silly Sports

Is it keeping warm? Yes, and fit too . . .

65

It's a penguin skipping!

These activities range from the daft to the downright dangerous – but you'll need to do some mental gymnastics to work out which is which . . .

what is this?

Does it warn ships? No, it just dives straight in . . .

It's a duck doing backstroke!

68

Is he tired? Probably, this is hard work . . .

It's a weightlifting mouse!

Does it say 'Tweet! Tweet!'? More like 'Wooooo-oah!' ...

It's a ghost doing a somersault on a skateboard!

Does it waddle? No, but it wobbles . . .

It's a rhino doing a headstand!

what is this?

Has it fallen asleep? More like fallen over . . .

It's a bird crashed out on a pool ball!

Does it have a hairy nose? Maybe, but definitely warm toes . . .

It's a boxer knitting a sock!

Does it go 'Boing!'? More like 'Oink!' ...

It's a hang-gliding pig!

74

Is it waving? Or drowning?...

It's a sinking canoe!

Funny Food

Does it go on your hand? . . . It goes everywhere! . . .

A cockerel in a chimney?

BOOM!

It's an explosion in a blancmange factory!

You'd need the taste buds of a celebrity chef to find some of these dishes appealing.

Bon appetit!

what is this?

Does it hold tea? Maybe with its trunk . . .

It's an elephant hiding behind an enormous bun!

80

Does it require good aim? It certainly does ...

It's a fried egg being eaten with chopsticks!

what is this?

Would it be good at a barbecue? Well, sort of . . .

It's a chef hiding in a sack!

82

Victory roll? No, a different sort . . .

It's worms carrying a Swiss roll home!

Do they become frogs? If you make a wish . . .

eyeballs?

It's an aerial view of a birthday cake!

Does it eat grass? It prefers sausages . . .

It's Dad losing control of the barbecue!

what is this?

Think there's nothing lucky about this? Too right...

It's an explosion in a pea soup factory!

Angry? No, hungry . . .

It's ants holding a biscuit!

An obstacle course? The most dangerous kind! . . . .

It's shark-infested custard!

Does it like cheese? Try another dairy product . . .

It's a canary eating an ice cream!

what is this?

Is it hot? Well, it was . . .

It's a seagull who's eaten a curry!

Is it on a long stick? No – but it's something sticky . . .

It's a spider doing a handstand on a honey pot!

Does it taste nice? You'll have to ask him . . .

It's a man diving into a vat of custard!

A road sign? Or a sign of greed?

It's a duck with a square cracker stuffed in her beak!

Household Oddjects

Did he sneeze? Quite likely . . .

It's a bird falling off a pepper pot!

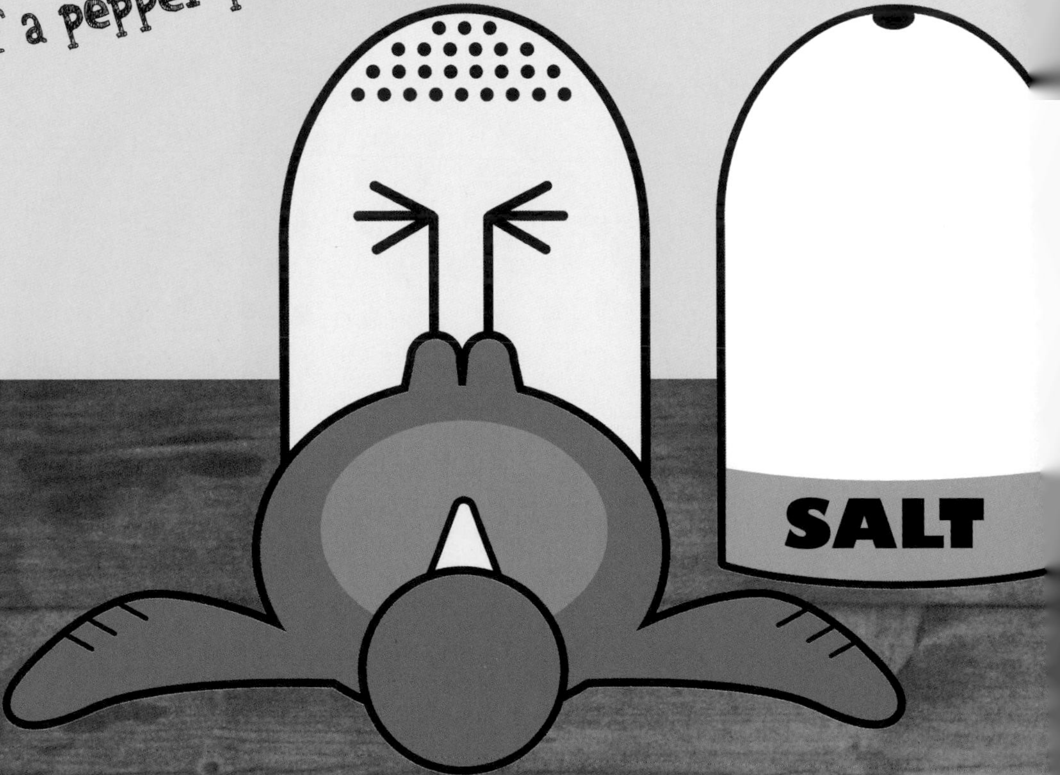

Chores would never be a
bore with these items.

Can you find some
ordinary household
objects in these rather
extraordinary images?

Does it go 'Boo!'? More like 'Hiss!' ...

It's a shirt's-eye view of a steam iron!

a ~~pointy~~ pepper pot?

Warning: Poisonous? They could be . . . .

It's two spiders at the bottom of a mop bucket!

What is this?

Is it from an ancient tomb? More like your living room . . .

It's a cat peeping through the blinds!

Is it saying 'Ahhh'? Maybe — it does look relaxed . . .

It's a rabbit in a bath!

Round and pointy? No, round and round . . .

It's three rabbits in a tumble dryer!

Is it a creepy crawly? Just creepy, really . . .

It's a ghost on an ironing board!

103

Is it sleepy? It looks like it . . .

It's an ant tucked up in bed!

Is it sweet? Well, she is pretty cute . . .

It's a rabbit sitting on a plant pot.

Does it move slowly? Probably, that's quite heavy . . .

It's a superhero carrying a roll of carpet!

Does it have antennae? Yes, on its head . . .

It's an ant using a laptop!

what is this?

Is it for cooking? Not really . . . .

It's a tulip growing out of a dustbin!

109

what is this?

Is that its nose? No, its tongue...

It's a snake being sucked up by a vacuum cleaner!

Lovely lashes? No, but you see through it . . . .

It's a zebra outside a window!

Tricky Tech

Is it made of folded paper?

a paving slab
topped with custard?

113

It's a canary with an ereader!

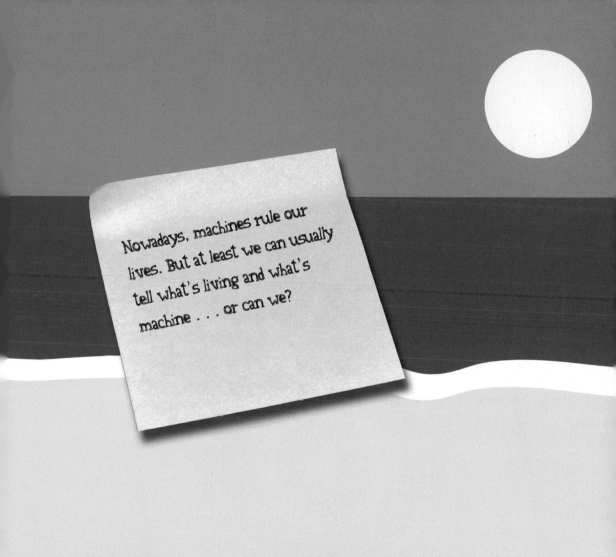

Nowadays, machines rule our lives. But at least we can usually tell what's living and what's machine . . . or can we?

what is this?

Is it a kind of road sign? More like a lost traveller... It's a hang-glider landing in a paddling pool!

Does it store data? Yes, all night long . . .

It's a robot in a sleeping bag!

Does this have a stick in it? Only a gear stick . . .

It's a snake sliding underneath a car!

117

what is this?

Is he looking straight ahead? He needs to or he'll crash! . . . It's a stick man on a bicycle!

118

Is this just a load of lines? Yes, basslines . . . .

It's a stick insect with an MP3 player!

Is this one hard to make out? He seems to think so! . . .

Is this a boxer peering at a tablet computer!

Is this breakfast? More like breakdance . . .

It's Humpty Dumpty wearing headphones!

Is it playing? Why yes! . . .

It's ice-hockey with a doughnut for a puck!

Is this image totally random? Only if she's pressed 'shuffle'...

It's a shark with an MP3 player!

Does it guide ships? Not if it can't download the app it needs . . . It's an octopus trying to get a phone signal!

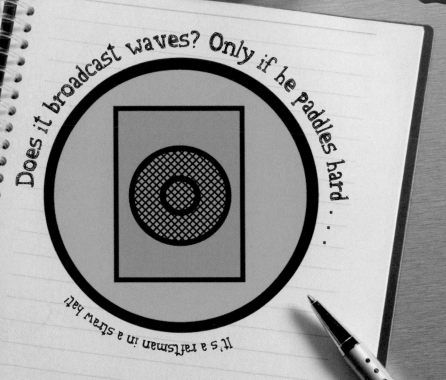

Does it broadcast waves? Only if he paddles hard . . .

It's a raftsman in a straw hat!

Is this situation going to blow up? Only if she wasn't invited . . . It's a snake entering an igloo!